How to Avoid Proposal Missteps

17 MISTAKES

That Broadcast Hidden Negative Messages

Which Dramatically Decrease Your

Federal Contract WIN Probability

A. L. Heisig

ISBN-13: 978-1466259072

ISBN-10: 1466259078

FOREWORD

"I am not remotely interested in just being good." - Vince Lombardi

The preparation process for responding to a federal government Request For Proposal (RFP) or other solicitation begins long before final solicitation release. No contractor, at least no contractor in his right mind, goes into that long and often expensive process to lose. However, as painful as the thought might be, the simple statistical truth is that when there is to be a single contract awarded, all but one of the proposals are losers. With that in mind, each contractor must do everything within his power to improve his odds of success: to be that one WINNER.

This book provides concise, insightful perspectives on how to avoid pitfalls when developing a proposal in response to a government requirement and enhance a company's "WIN" probability.

Proposal preparation procedures vary from company to company according to the internal proposal controls they implement during proposal creation. Some contractors have established on-call support teams for proposal preparation. Others approach each acquisition individually, and still others have teams, which only do proposal preparation. Whichever approach a contractor takes, the objective is creating, refining, and submitting a winning proposal that simultaneously attains as many business objectives as possible.

Proposal preparation is an expensive proposition, and is not undertaken lightly. Most government acquisition personnel have little insight into the costs of proposal preparation on an individual basis. However, they do recognize that taken together the costs run into the hundreds of millions of dollars annually.

This book is a valuable reference tool. In this brilliantly concise book, A. L. Heisig succinctly describes how to identify and avoid 17 proposal errors that may indeed be sinking a company's reputation and decreasing its WIN probability and ties them into leadership issues that could be the cause. How to Avoid Proposal Missteps is valuable to beginning employees as well as seasoned executives.

Lenn Vincent, RADM, USN (RET). Industry Chair at the Defense Acquisition University and Independent Consultant

A. L. Heisig

ACKNOWLEDGMENTS

This book would not be possible without the generous time and effort given by professionals from both sides of the federal business opportunity equation: the contracting professionals of the federal government and the business leaders of industry. Contracting professionals seek the best companies to carry out the missions of federal government agencies. They view proposals through the lens of comparative value. Business leaders view proposals from the context of business continuity and growth. They continually need to justify the return on investment for maintaining the overhead required to produce winning proposals. I thank all of these professionals for their valuable time and for the insight and perspectives which they have provided.

I am grateful for the intellectual contribution of the Association of Proposal Management Professionals for standardizing and elevating the process of competitive business acquisition. They inspired me in following their mission to advance the arts, sciences, and technologies of new business acquisition and to promote the professionalism of those engaged in those pursuits.

I am deeply appreciative for the help of my editor, several friends, colleagues, and family members.

The insightful assistance of my supportive and creative wife, Sandi, is evidenced throughout the book. Her keen eye for detail and impact weaves throughout this book.

Dear Successful Business Owner,

You may be scuttling your business reputation, and losing potential contracts, and be unaware of the cause. Are you:

Looking at a robust business development pipeline with meager contract wins?

Wondering why your federal government proposals seldom make the cut?

A proposal is the most powerful communication you can provide to your potential customer. Is yours working for or against you?

Your proposal is required reading on the part of those who make the purchasing decisions. It responds to their expressly identified needs. Reading your solution is in the government's best interest since it provides potential resolutions to their needs. The government wants a winner. Are you really in the game or not?

> *Your proposal is your official representation of your corporate ability to interpret requirements and perform tasks.*

Find out what many other successful companies already know: how to avoid elimination and shape perceptions in their favor.

This book highlights common proposal errors, potential motivations causing errors and the corporate situations that foster them. The solutions relate to four leadership and management principles: plan, organize, direct and control. Eliminate errors in these areas and prevent poor perceptions of your company.

Enhance your company's proud reputation, and yours!

In Anticipation of Your Much Greater Success.

A. L. Heisig

A. L. Heisig

INTRODUCTION

Submit or die. If your business supports the federal government, you must submit proposals. Talking to many contracting professionals over the years has revealed some common shortfalls in the thousands of proposals they evaluate. These seventeen frequent, *AND PREVENTABLE,* errors appear repeatedly. The inevitable result is a poor perception of the proposal submitting companies. Your proposals are evaluated and scored on many factors including risk perceptions. Evaluators almost universally assign more risk to companies they perceive poorly from presented proposals. Thus, those companies' scores fall short.

Someone else gets the contract!

Your proposal evaluation is based on two separate but intertwined processes. These processes are not secrets. They have their roots in human nature. They are carried out by evaluators' individual interactions within a structured decision making process. They are the most powerful processes affecting your success probability when you submit a proposal.

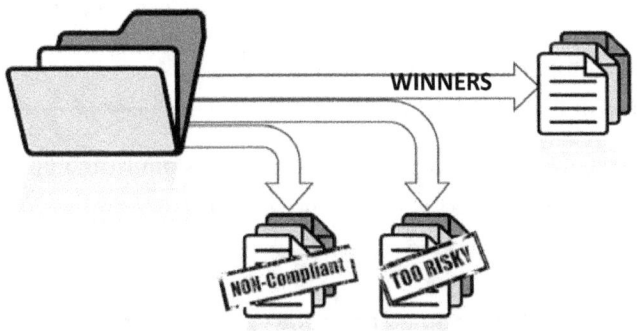

1. The first process **culls proposals**. The evaluation team evaluates proposals for noncompliance and eliminates those responses immediately from further consideration.

DO NOT HELP THEM ELIMINATE YOU FROM COMPETITION BY PROPOSAL NONCOMPLIANCE!

2. The second process assigns objective scores that are based on presented facts and verifiable evidence, which are then weighted by risk-based perceptions.

HELP THEM FORM A WINNING PERCEPTION OF YOUR COMPANY!

In a close competition, evaluators will be looking for ever finer details in order to make value judgments about the relative merits of proposals. They are looking for companies to eliminate. Your proposal must be ironclad all the way to the end.

DON'T LET AN ACCUMULATION OF PROPOSAL ERRORS TAKE YOU OUT AT THE ENDGAME!

These 17 common proposal errors impact the government's (your client's) perception of you, your team, and your company's ability to perform on a government contract.

> *Each of these proposal errors can be avoided by leadership actions.*

These errors have motivational root causes or stem from internal corporate conditions. Solutions to these errors come from excellent leadership and progressive management.

Train your team and manage your proposal process. Eliminate these 17 errors before they negatively affect your business reputation.[1]

---

1 See Attachment A for a quick list of all 17 errors

CONTENTS

PART 1 - ERRORS INDICATING DIRECTIONLESS LEADERSHIP

Mental multitasking is NOT necessarily a virtue. A fundamental principle of a government solicitation is focus. The response to the solicitation, your proposal, should demonstrate a similar focus. That focus includes both responding to all of the requirements of the solicitation and providing an easily understood linkage to the promise of rich benefits to the government by your selection as the best choice to perform on the contract.

A truly coherent and encompassing message resonates to all parts of the government's needs. A lack of focus shows a failure to understand what it takes to perform the contract successfully.

 The absence of coherency subliminally leads the evaluation team to feel that the company submitting the proposal is not focused on the job at hand. This feeling in turn raises doubts about the leadership the company plans to put in charge of executing the contract.

Subsequently, the evaluation will presume greater risk with your company, and this greater risk assessment dooms your proposal to a lower evaluation score.

Your Proposal's Lack of a Coherent Message

Perceived Lack of Leadership Direction at Your Company

Lowered Confidence in Your Corporate Ability to Execute a Contract

Greater Risk Assigned to Your Company's Proposal

Low Evaluation Score

Disregarding Sun Tzu

You and your team have just made a gut-wrenching decision. You have committed to spend precious bid and proposal money in an effort to win a government contract. The solicitation requirements fit your corporate sweet spot. Your team has generated a compelling case. You are confident their ideas have merit. Your pricing is competitive. Your team understands the requirements. All vectors seem aligned in your favor. Your thoughts rise above the details that go into winning a government contract. Departing the Go/No-Go meeting, you ask your proposal manager for a quick meeting in your office. You ask a question:

Do we truly understand our proposal evaluators?

Error #1

Not truly

understanding your

audience

Almost invariably a government team is put together to evaluate all responses from several perspectives. Typically, evaluators come from a variety of organizational backgrounds. Each one evaluating your proposal has a different perspective. Evaluators also have different roles.

1. The Source Selection Authority (SSA)

2. The Source Selection Evaluation Board (SSEB)

3. The Contracting Officer (CO)

Have you accounted for their perceptions as well as the solicitation details?

Understand evaluators' mindsets and direct your team to write to each evaluator according to their role and perspectives.

The SSA has the highest-level perspective, and selects and justifies the winning proposal. The SSEB examines the details, weighs the merits, and makes a recommendation to the SSA. The CO ensures that the acquisition rules and regulations are observed within a proposal. His or her charter is to ensure a responsible and justifiable contract award.

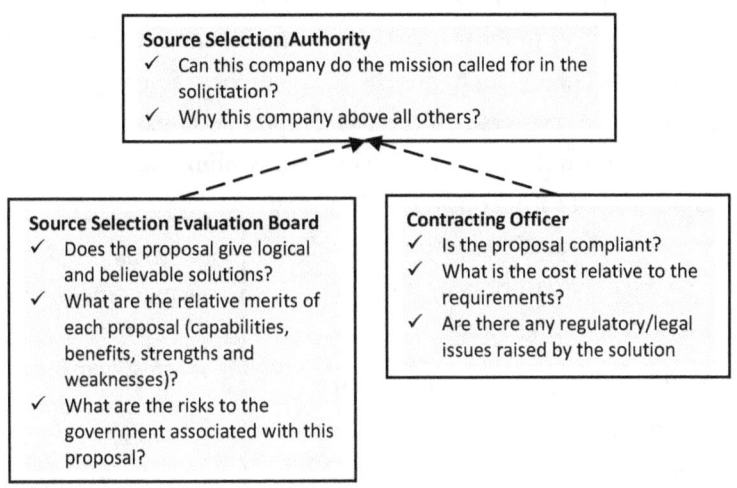

Source Selection Authority
✓ Can this company do the mission called for in the solicitation?
✓ Why this company above all others?

Source Selection Evaluation Board
✓ Does the proposal give logical and believable solutions?
✓ What are the relative merits of each proposal (capabilities, benefits, strengths and weaknesses)?
✓ What are the risks to the government associated with this proposal?

Contracting Officer
✓ Is the proposal compliant?
✓ What is the cost relative to the requirements?
✓ Are there any regulatory/legal issues raised by the solution

The proposal you submit normally contains several volumes. This often includes an executive summary, which is the overall perspective of your offer. There will be technical and/or management volumes that give the details of your response to the various requirements put forth in the solicitation. Often a past performance volume is required, illustrating that your qualifications are relevant to the solicitation. The cost volume communicates your price proposal to the financial analysts and cost evaluators. The contracting volume or section provides your response to the contracting context requirements.

Write the executive summary to the mindset of the Source Selection Authority. The SSA has a unique responsibility to view the contract through the lens of the agency mission that the resulting contract will support. The SSA's perspective is to answer two fundamental questions:

1. *Is this company capable of doing the work?*

2. *Why this company above all others?*

The recommendation of the SSEB and the CO assist him in answering these two questions. Your executive summary is your suggested answer to those questions. Write it at an executive level. It should reflect fact, not hype. The SSA will form a perception of your company's professionalism based upon your executive summary. This influences your chances of winning this solicitation, and future ones! The SSA may only read the executive summary and it may be the only part of your proposal read by every SSEB member.

> *Evaluators are human. They have different professional roles and therefore different perspectives.*

Write the technical, past performance, and managerial volumes for the SSEB members. How do members of an SSEB view themselves? Many government employees view themselves as highly competent, underappreciated, and undercompensated with a monumental workload. The government chooses proposal evaluators for their expertise.

Each SSEB member usually has another primary job. Consequently, their motivations might differ from what you may expect. Board members are assigned extra duties—to read and evaluate one or more sections of proposals—in addition to their existing pressing demands. They want to get past this distraction and get back to their job. However, they also want to give a professional review of each proposal.

Their conflicting motivations influence how they react to your proposal. Their first action will be to reduce the proposal evaluation workload. Figuratively, they have loaded the big guns and are scanning the proposal horizon to shoot down easy targets first. They will be looking to find those proposals they can easily eliminate.

They dispose of unsophisticated proposals by spotting simple compliance errors. They then turn their attention to the surviving proposals. Evaluators more favorably perceive companies that successfully portray themselves as capable of accurately completing the solicitation tasks. Even at this early stage, they will start to form perceptions of proposals that seem risky while scanning for compliance errors.

Write the cost volume and contracting sections to the Contracting Officer. The CO makes sure that any contract resulting from your proposal complies with the numerous rules and regulations governing contracting. The contracting officer makes a risk evaluation against cost after he or she receives the technical and managerial input. The CO presents the risk-correlated findings of all compliant proposals with his recommendation for award to the SSA for consideration.

Many different evaluators will see various parts of your proposal during the evaluation. Direct your proposal team to understand and write to resonate with each evaluation team member's role and perspective.

TIP: Think mindsets, not functions, when you write.

The Distorted Lens

The water's surface above a tropical coral reef is enticing. You gaze expectantly toward the shadowy shapes that dart below the surface in a mosaic of mysterious montages. In an effort to get a clearer appreciation, you put on your snorkel facemask and peer just beneath the surface. Immediately the colors are brighter. The movements are distinct and the picture of life in the sea becomes vividly comprehensible. A convincing executive summary similarly acts as the enabler showing an immediate clear understanding of the picture of your proposal.

Error #2
Failure to succinctly answer why YOUR company above all others

Failure to have a convincing, focused executive summary obscures your corporate capability with a distorted lens of unfocused details. Without a perspective illuminating why your company should be considered above all others, evaluators naturally tend toward a mindset of believing you have an unclear understanding of your intended course toward satisfying their mission objectives.

An executive summary serves two purposes. It highlights your company's Unique Qualifications and Capabilities (UQC) for this specific proposal. Additionally, it ties the entire proposal together when the other volumes of the proposal are split up for the various technical, managerial, and cost evaluation teams. The entire proposal must reinforce your cogently stated corporate UQC in the executive summary.

Writing to the government is not about hype. If your submission is hype with no substance, it will adversely portray your company.

Sophisticated proposals educate and reduce the perception of risk in the minds of decision makers. Each evaluation team member is by default a decision maker. Proposal writing must be positive and professional to be convincing.

When should you construct an executive summary? A draft executive summary should be one of the earliest activities, after initial planning, in developing a proposal. The author, preferably the lead sales person for the opportunity, writes the first draft of the executive summary prior to the rest of the proposal.

The sales lead captures the customer's major requirements and links them to your company's unique qualifications and ability to solve the problems. The draft executive summary is used to brief the proposal team at kickoff to orient everyone to the thematic thread of the proposal. The document is then updated through the proposal development process as the details of the solution are developed and justified in response to each specific solicitation requirement. Done well, this practice creates a document that encapsulates the core of the entire proposal during composition.

> *Writing the executive summary is a key part of the proposal preparation process.*

Some small proposals use the executive summary as a stand in for a storyboard of the proposal. This is not a recommended practice. It helps to keep the writers oriented with a kind of synopsized overview, but fails to deliver the benefits of ensuring compliance with the solicitation, assist in planning and organizing sections, documentation of win themes, benefits and discriminators and ensuring that a unified message is communicated throughout the proposal.

A well written executive summary is also useful to brie senior management, internal staff, partners and subcontractors and in some cases external customers, where permitted.

The executive summary should evolve in concert with the entire proposal. In cases where an executive summary is not permitted, a well-crafted cover letter or volume lead in sections can serve the purpose. The executive summary should be continuously reviewed and endorsed by top management as it is written for the government decision makers as a "stand alone" document.

Writing an executive summary is integral to the overall proposal process. Corporate leadership must ensure that organizational control and the appropriate checks and balances are applied.

> **TIP: You are writing the executive summary primarily for the Source Selection Authority. Focus on how your proposal will uniquely benefit the agency mission.**
>
> **TIP: <u>AWAYS</u> include an executive summary, even if only in an e-mail proposal submission transmission.**

Iron Chef Myopia

Cooking contest television shows pit various culinary contestants against one another. Under the rules of the show, individuals, or small groups, compete while commentary and analysis are given for the benefit of the audience. These performances showcase talent while providing education and entertainment.

Works of gastronomic delight are finally submitted to a panel of judges. The judges have established criteria to evaluate the prepared dishes. Invariably, some less sophisticated contestants prepare dishes that shortchange the very criteria upon which success depends!

Error #3

Failure to weight evaluation criteria properly

Government solicitations provide success criteria. The evaluation factors for award (Section M) of a federal government solicitation provide the proposal evaluation criteria. This section normally contains various criteria that are prioritized and weighted. See Appendix A for the uniform federal contract format.

SSEB members have explicit instructions about evaluation criteria before commencing their proposal evaluations. This becomes the objective framework for SSEB mindsets.

Present the facts in your proposal in a way that addresses the perspectives of different audiences. Weave the benefits relating to the RFP Section M criteria into your entire proposal. Address what is most meaningful to the SSEB members' evaluation criteria throughout your response. The evaluators will associate your corporate ability, consciously and subconsciously, against the evaluation criteria.

The initiation of the evaluation criteria into the solicitation response starts with the core proposal writing team. The criteria influence the response strategy, outline structuring, page count allocation, past performance selections, and guidance to cost volume managers. Integrate the evaluation criteria at this early step. Otherwise, all other information will not persuasively influence the evaluation.

Whether you organize with a storyboard, a proposal development worksheet, a sales proposal planner, or some other method, the evaluation criteria must be part of your directed guidance. Your directions must flow to writers, editors, and reviewers. They serve as guideposts during the proposal development process.

Some writers get so involved in communicating the technical details that they forget why they are writing in the first place. They are in a competition! Just as in any other team activity, each member of your proposal team has his or her innate strengths. Consistently align the team with the overall solicitation objectives or the entire effort will usually result in failure. Your corporate reputation will then take a bruising and start to sink, due to factors entirely within your control.

Include evaluation criteria into the earliest strategy formulations.

Transitioning from an outline, a storyboard or other directions into formal, professional writing is often the hardest task for a writer. This is particularly true for technical personnel who are not accustomed to proposal writing. A core team member, usually a volume manager, should conduct focused, one-on-one direction with writers at the beginning of their writing assignments.

Provide guidance! Explain the core team's thinking and how the evaluation criteria should appear, or be expressed, in the writer's draft. Proposal creation should be an interactive activity among team members. Proposal guidance should stimulate the writer's imagination, implant the significance of the evaluation criteria, and put it into a context which a the technical writer can internalize.

TIP: Keep guidance simple and relevant to the specific context of each proposal effort.

PART 2 - ERRORS SIGNIFYING POOR ORGANIZATION

Examples sell! The government expects a winning company will organize itself and provide orderly delivery of the goods and services. That expectation will be either bolstered or diminished by their perceptions of your ability to organize properly to produce a proposal. Your proposal team should have clear lines of responsibility and accountability for every proposal task. Your proposal reflects your company's organizational competence.

The errors described in this chapter start to introduce doubt in the mindset of evaluators about the organizational capabilities of your company. Thus, a significant element of risk is introduced into the overall evaluation rating.

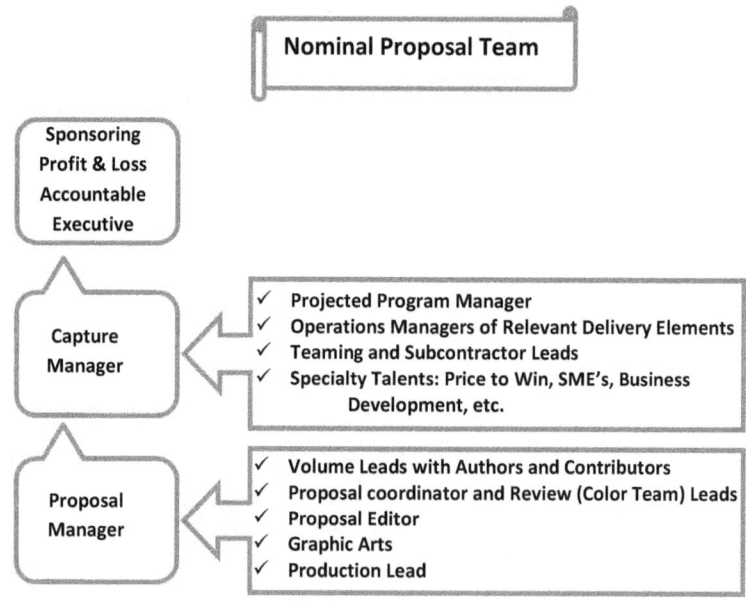

Nominal Proposal Team

Sponsoring Profit & Loss Accountable Executive

Capture Manager
- ✓ Projected Program Manager
- ✓ Operations Managers of Relevant Delivery Elements
- ✓ Teaming and Subcontractor Leads
- ✓ Specialty Talents: Price to Win, SME's, Business Development, etc.

Proposal Manager
- ✓ Volume Leads with Authors and Contributors
- ✓ Proposal coordinator and Review (Color Team) Leads
- ✓ Proposal Editor
- ✓ Graphic Arts
- ✓ Production Lead

Amateur Hour

Amateurs fail to plan because it takes time. Professionals take the time to plan, and succeed. Effective written communication is the core of professional proposals. Failure to write clearly and honestly, while satisfying the reader's expectation of completeness, order, and structural integrity, puts your business reputation at risk. If your proposal fails in this critical expectation, your proposal is viewed as amateurish, as is your company.

Professionals organize. Someone must be in charge.

The person in charge, called the proposal manager, should organize the effort for maximum professional results. A good proposal outline is vital to proper proposal organization. The proposal manager should break up the solicitation into its constituent elements. Those elements form a rough proposal outline for the core proposal team members. Team members should annotate the pertinent items for their sections to assist in preparing a detailed outline.

Error #4

Unprofessional writing

These actions serve dual purposes. It requires the proposal manager to identify core team members and notify them of duties early in the process. It also mentally prepares proposal team section leaders and prepares their minds for the task ahead.

Planning a professional proposal must include preparing a detailed outline, determining an achievable schedule, and providing adequate guidelines. For each outlined section, designate the estimated page count and section team leader.

In addition to a detailed structure for constructing the proposal, the outline should be accompanied by a writers guide package with instructions prominently affixed with task assignments. Assemble common items into the writers guide. Include schedules, key words or ideas, font size, page margins, anathema words or phrases relative to this particular customer, and similar instructions. [1] This is the proposal manager's chance to provide contextual and technical guidance tailored to each specific RFP or solicitation.

The proposal manager must possess the control authority corresponding to his or her responsibility to produce winning proposals. Professional writing control includes a clearly understood method to manage assignments, report progress, identify areas of compliance and deficiency. These methods must be accompanied by the means to direct quality and deadline compliance. Review processes, commonly called color team reviews, are part of the methodology, but are by no means sufficient. Some companies have elaborate checkpoints called gate reviews, which mirror

Professional proposal preparation demands a clear and repeatable

government major program decision process methodologies. Others have internal progress milestones based upon commercial practices. Appendix B includes some progress milestones that various companies consider. Professional proposal preparation demands a repeatable and clearly understood methodology.

Effective proposal writing is a creative communications art. It brings an original, compelling inventiveness to a unique set of parameters. Your proposals should persuade the evaluators that your company could BEST perform the tasks in the solicitation.

1 See Attachment B for a suggested set of minimum elements to include in a proposal writers guide

Proposal writing does not suspend grammar rules nor is it slavish to them. Stylistically, your proposal should be in the same voice, have correct tenses and, most of all, reveal continuity of thought and orderly purpose.

The entire document construction should flow together as a coherent persuasive entity. It convinces the reader that your unique solution exhibits the best characteristics, value, and lowest risk.

Persuasive writing in proposals is not about propaganda or hype. It's about proving your case. You must substantiate your convincing statements with logic and evidence. Present the required elements in an appropriate, relevant context. A proposal is not writing primarily about your company. Your solution

> *Proposal writing is about the government's requirements and how your company can best perform to meet them.*

to the government's requirements are the raison d'être for the document. You are proving that your solution is the best value and your company is the best choice to implement this solution. This difference is lost on many unsophisticated companies.

It's all about the CUSTOMER!

Your communications illustrate your understanding of the requirements in clear, concise language. Using jargon is usually a mistake. The technical evaluation team will expect a professional tone and they read many proposals in sequence. Excessive jargon can be glaring. Some evaluators may feel pandered to by jargon. What may seem natural to your team might be downright annoying. If you need to use some jargon, include definitions in an appendix.

Some companies find themselves in a personnel resource quandary during periods of high volume proposal activity. Every company has limited professional talent to apply to the opportunities they choose to pursue. A rigorous and dispassionate capture management process will focus on the best opportunities. A key management decision is how to select which opportunities to resource with existing talent. Companies forgo some great opportunities due to in-house resource constraints.

Rather than miss opportunities, a preferable option is to contract with professional talent, on a case-by-case basis, to fill gaps when proposals demand more assets than are available in-house. This option has a high return on investment. The immediate costs are known. The long-term costs are nil. Expenditures are clearly identifiable to the task, and the results are high quality from well-qualified consultants.

> **TIP: Provide a proposal writers guide to the subcontractors providing input to your proposal.**

> **TIP: Understand the situation or conditions that generated the RFP requirements. It becomes much easier to describe convincingly your company's capabilities to meet those requirements.**

Parrots Are Seldom Intellectual Icons

A tutor often uses reiterative feedback as a tool for memorization. The context is information value transfer from tutor to student. The student is usually not capable of expanding the discourse's intellectual value. Responding to a government solicitation is not a tutor/student relationship. It is a subject matter expert endeavor providing intellectual added value.

The government expects to receive good value from the contract. Your proposal should convince the government that your company is the best choice to perform on this contract. In your proposal, don't merely parrot the words in the RFP or solicitation. The government knows what the solicitation says. They wrote it.

Error #5

Not providing a unique, compelling solution

Parroting will brand your company with the unenviable reputation of not having the requisite experience or not being a serious contender for this RFP. If your company *is* a novice in government contracting, get professional assistance.

Evaluators perceive your company as risky if it merely reiterates the words of the solicitation. The government will perceive your company as providing no meaningful value.

There is a myth harbored in some companies that a good strategy is to feed back words in your proposal almost exactly as written in the RFP. Nothing is further from the truth. Your professional reputation can hardly nosedive faster than with this unsophisticated strategy. If you believe in this myth, I offer you a seat on the next scheduled UFO abduction voyage. Procurement officers want to do business with a professional company that knows what they are doing. They evaluate your company in part on your ability to communicate professionally.

Amateurishly repeating the words from the RFP does not form the right contexts, for *your* company, for *this specific RFP*. Winners state concisely the features and benefits of a compelling solution.

The solution to the RFP requirement is not rote recitation. When your company provides a unique, compelling solution, you rise above your competition.

Sometimes a proposal becomes an RFP recitation when the proposal manager isn't adequately supported. Without experienced help, he or she is required to write without the clear and valuable inputs required to make the proposal a success. Mindless solicitation cut and paste regurgitation can become his or her default position. This can deep six your corporate reputation.

> *Concisely highlight your solution's compelling benefits.*

Your proposal team must include sufficient qualified technical talent to provide meaningful solutions to the RFP requirements. The close examination and analysis of your experts should then translate into a wealth of meaningful proposal inputs. Align inputs to the work breakdown structure created by your proposal team. Crafting these inputs into a coherent and compelling description of how you plan to execute what the government needs and the benefits of your plan is a hallmark of an organized, competent company. Enhance your reputation with professionalism rather than damage it with a clearly inferior proposal.

TIP: Write to the RFP, but never merely reiterate.

Being Unfriended

Relationships matter is a tag line for a popular online professional networking service. When you wish to invite someone into an online professional relationship, you choose from a series of existing shared background relationships as a basis for extending the invitation. The underlying rationale for this choice is to establish in the mind of the recipient that you are truly a friend. It then follows that each can have trusted online dialogs.

Each past performance example cited in your proposal must list a reference point of contact (POC). The POC is the person that the proposal has listed for the Source Selection Evaluation Board to contact to validate your company's past performance in contracts which you have identified as roughly similar to the work contained in the solicitation.

Error #6

Not validating past performance points of contact

Make sure that each person referenced is currently willing to give your company a good recommendation.

Contacts have many reasons for giving (or not providing) good past performance recommendations. These reasons may not be based on anything to do with your actual performance.

- They may simply have forgotten that your company did the work.

- They may never give a good recommendation to anyone as a matter of principle or policy.

- They may have a personal situation that may taint their perception of the entire contract and, by association, your company.

A reference POC can be one of a variety of people associated with the contract. The most senior person with knowledge of the contract(s) and with a favorable impression of your company's performance is your best choice. A government contracting POC is preferable.

A commercial contract can be a good reference in the absence of a comparable government contract, but other complicating factors can arise. Your once excellent commercial customer may now be your competitor resulting from buyouts, acquisitions, joint ventures, and mergers. Many government RFP's require corporate organizational change histories and explanations for commercial contract references.

The organizational change history clarifies ownership and business relationships for evaluators. In essence, it tracks the performing unit from one corporate entity to distinguish who actually performed work on a cited contract.

Some businesses have internal policies prohibiting providing any corporate performance recommendations for other companies. Some companies have a corporate policy to submit only bland statements indicating that a specific contract was held and completed.

Who should make contact to verify a POC's willingness to give your company a good recommendation? The request is personal, as well as, organizational. You are making a business request, but also a request outside of their normal job scope. Your senior person with the most direct relationship with the POC should make the call.

Your nominated point of contact may or may not be contacted during the government's due diligence process. However, validation contacts are quite common in today's competitive environment.

If requested to give an evaluation of your company's performance, the nature of the response will depend in large measure upon the point of contact's current state of mind. Reinforce good recollections of your highly regarded past performance. The POC's most recent emotion associated with your company will be the one most likely conveyed.

> *Verify each cited reference person's willingness to give a good recommendation early in the proposal preparation process.*

Your proposal team should personally alert a nominated POC early in the past performance selection process before you list him or her as a reference. Then follow up with your contact within two weeks of the proposal submission date. The first POC contact ensures that you select past performance contracts with a good reference before you invest time writing. The second contact verifies that the POC is still in the listed management position and that the proper emotional legacy is foremost in his or her mind.

Always take the time, shortly before submission, to make sure that each POC you have listed is still your friend.

TIP: Call or visit the person. Do not use e-mail. You want to generate a vivid, personal, and positive memory of your company and its performance.

PART 3 - ERRORS DEMONSTRATING LACK OF CONTROL

Predictable high quality results don't happen by accident. You must control the proposal preparation process. After you get the process under control, you must monitor the quality of the output. Companies that consistently win do both of these things very well.

The evidence of an out-of-control company is a disjointed, poor quality proposal. Lack of effective proposal process control promotes elemental errors. These errors equate to more contract performance risk in the minds of the evaluators. The mental image of your business acumen deteriorates and the loss of contracts results.

When All Else Fails, Read the Directions

Remember the stories? A father frenetically struggling to assemble complex toys on Christmas eve. Movie scenes highlighting bumbling parents attempting outwardly simple tasks and failing miserably. Consumers suspiciously eyeing cardboard cartons with *some assembly required* written inconspicuously in tiny print. The frantic last minute scramble to find directions.

Winning proposals is not about sending in thoughtless, error-filled submissions. Producing winning proposals is not a mind numbing, repetitive assembly line process either, although there are certainly good processes to follow. Treat each solicitation individually with rigorous analytic thought and careful attention to detail.

Error #7

Not responding to specific directions in the proposal

The government wants something. The solicitation tells you what they want, and the contracting officer tells you how to respond to the solicitation.

Respond exactly to each requirement in Section L.

This section explicitly tells you what the contracting officer wants to see in the proposal. This may seem self evident, but a surprisingly large number of solicitation responses don't follow provided instructions. These become noncompliant and are among those evaluators throw out first. This self-generated error often appears when several disconnected proposal segments are boilerplate cut and pastes from previous proposals without validating the content applicability for the current RFP. This can occur in last minute attempts to "throw it over the transom" and the instruction details are overlooked.

Why does this happen? Perhaps some core team members believe they know best and don't have to pay close attention. They think, "Hey, it's just like the last one I wrote." It may be a feeling that it's someone else's job to make all the details fit. This indicates both a poorly controlled team and process.

Everyone on the proposal team should read the entire solicitation. The time it takes will pay off. Reading the entire proposal also establishes strong proposal process management control in the proposal team's collective consciousness.

Format your proposal following the structure provided in Section L of the RFP.

The overall proposal structure is formatted; however, some areas trip up the unwary. Some proposals eliminate or combine commonly expected sections. Others request information in multiple places to facilitate government evaluation. If you neglect to be rigorous about this formatting, you indicate that you do not follow directions well. Formatting

> *Establish controls early in the proposal process.*

failure flies a red flag about your company's ability to perform the contract competently.

Don't get me wrong. There is a structure to all government proposals. However, the structure is flexible underneath the overall solicitation outlines, and those differences can be subtle. In some cases, you may alter the structure of your response due to the differences. Intelligent control is a critical professional responsibility.

You may have proposal-support software. That's great! Proposal software assistance can help you in many ways, but preconceived solutions are not a viable substitute for conscientious and diligent management control. Make sure that your proposal follows the exact structure the contracting officer requested in each solicitation. This also helps when a large proposal evaluation team engages experts for one specific technical concept. The same information is contained in the same place in each proposal. If your proposal does it differently than directed, it will be perceived as failing to address adequately all of the requirements.

For responses to individual task orders related to Indefinite Delivery, Indefinite Quantity (IDIQ) contracts there can be significant format variations. Consider each task order RFP as an entirely new solicitation. It just builds on the foundations given in the master contract. The master contract may have specified formats for task order responses.

Usually, format errors in IDIQ task order submissions are failures to follow instructions in the master contract, as well as, all instructions relative to each new task order.

Management control must be in place to review each part of each submission conscientiously and thoroughly. This applies to contract submissions and task order submissions.

TIP: Everyone on the team should read the entire solicitation, including references. In the long run, it will help avoid errors.

Ten Pounds in a Five Pound Bag

When cooking, be creative. When baking, stick to the recipe. Adding novel or exotic extra baking ingredients on the fly will result in soggy cake, charred cookies, or lumpy bread. Figuratively, while preparing government proposals, you cook your company's creative solutions, but you bake the proposal.

A government evaluation team tries to diminish its paperwork stack and concentrate on proposals truly worth examining closely. An easy method to clear the clutter is to discard those responses that exceed page counts.

Proposals with excessive page counts in some sections are quickly stamped NONCOMPLIANT. Some proposal evaluators will throw away any pages that are in excess of the limit. Now your carefully crafted logical reasoning is half finished, and your persuasive document disappears into a silent void. The whole section makes no sense at all.

Error #8

Exceeding page count limits

It sounds simple, but in practice, keeping to the page count while writing a hard-hitting, convincing, and compliant proposal is not easy. To adhere to the page count, some proposal writers default to merely stating the corporate interpretation of facts devoid of the context to provide a clear understanding. Thereafter, those proposals can meander into a meaningless mumble.

Avoiding this default reaction is another area where clear thought, professional capability, and experience shine. Your proposal is a sales document. It must convey, in a professional tone, your company's unique qualifications, capabilities and benefits with a convincing plan of action. It must illustrate that your team thoroughly understands the requirements. You must convince the evaluation team of your corporate capability to fulfill the solicitation requirements flawlessly and with the least risk.

Often, team inexperience leads directly to excessive page count. Excessive page counts are often a variation on a tired theme: "If I talk long enough, I'm sure to cover all bases."

To prevent this problem, make sure your proposal team is fully aware of the page count limits stated in the RFP. However, you must avoid restricting your proposal writing team's ability to provide all essential information needed to properly construct a meaningful response.

Draft addendums can be useful in balancing the competing objectives of page limits and providing adequate information to volume leaders. Your proposal manager should tell writers to deliver an initial draft to the required page count, but put into addendums any additional information that the writer feels would improve the response. The proposal manager should decide what is most important.

Generate writing guidelines and make sure writers conform to them early in the process. Addenda allow writers to include information they consider significant into an

Publish writing guidelines for each proposal.

addendum for the proposal manager to consider. The proposal manager, your editor in chief, now has the flexibility to evaluate inputs from a broader perspective than could individual authors.

TIP: Storyboard an annotated outline. Ensure the page counts are correct for each section.

Unfair Advantages

Don't hand an unfair advantage to your competition. An entire industry has evolved regarding Price-To-Win as a subset of competitive financial business intelligence. Companies specialize in ethical and comprehensive analysis of your competitors' pricing and costing practices. Many techniques, including research of publicly available financial records, analyzing your past winning proposals and industry data mining are used. They apply analysis with arcane and sophisticated mathematical formulas with more Greek letters than the *Iliad*. Imagine their delight when they find you have given them codes to unlock the information they seek so hard to derive. They are then in a position to take advantage of close approximations of your own cost/price models.

Error #9

Putting pricing related info into inappropriate volumes

Some proposal writers believe they can influence some technical and/or managerial evaluators with subtle price-related information included in volumes other than the pricing volume.

Don't do it.

This transparent and crude practice has two significant drawbacks. First, it does not follow solicitation directions. Second, it potentially reveals pricing information to competitors.

This error usually occurs when the volume or section writer believes that by including some price-related information in other volumes, they somehow create a value perception. What actually happens, if the information does not disqualify the proposal, is this price-related information becomes subject to the Freedom of Information Act (FOIA).

Pricing volumes are protected from public release under FOIA. Any pricing information located elsewhere in the proposal won't be redacted in FOIA disclosures. Using FOIA, many companies routinely request information relative to competitors' past contracts in a given field. They are looking to the future. If your team includes price related information in other than the pricing volume, you have created a competitive vulnerability. You have handed business competitive intelligence experts a gift-wrapped golden nugget.

> *Pricing information put into non-pricing volumes is not redacted in FOIA responses.*

Your current proposal is part of a continuum of competitions. Don't give future competitors a free ride. Allowing this pricing information to seep into other volumes damages your future competitive viability. Your credibility to the government for this and future contracts has similarly been tarnished.

TIP: Alert your editors to look for price-related information in inappropriate volumes. They are not often instructed to look for this type of error.

Spelling Sex When You Meant Six

An office worker was proudly described as being a *vast suppository of information*. A large city mayor was alleged to have forcefully stated *Let's get this straight. The police don't cause disorder. The police are here to preserve disorder.* We derive great amusement from malapropisms, the inadvertent, or seemingly inadvertent, use of words that sound similar to the words intended in the context of the sentence.

Your proposal is not an attempt to lighten the mood of an appreciative audience. You are creating a business response to a business issue. Inadvertent erroneous word usage will disrupt the serious intent of your document. Jarring interruption of your carefully planned flow of information is an unprofessional interruption in the important evaluation process. Catching these errors is important.

Error #10

Depending only upon spell-check to ensure correct grammar and usage

Spell-check is necessary, but not sufficient. You are communicating to a sophisticated, busy audience.

Check for spelling and grammatical errors.

These simple errors are distracting and annoying. They are also clear indications of your team's inattention to detail.

The management evaluation team will consider poor grammar an indication of a less professional, and hence more risky, company. This can influence their perspective of your corporate ability to perform on the contract.

Do not let your proposal team fall into intellectual lethargy. Spell-check and grammar-check are simply two helpful tools. They are NOT a total solution. A cold professional edit (one completed by someone who has not been associated with overall proposal preparation) should catch errors like: *sex* for *six*, *than* for *then*, *loose* for *lose* and so forth. Your proposal team is better served with a professional input rather than depending entirely on automated software checking.

The following list humorously illustrates items not normally caught by spell check systems or grammar-checking tools. They are extracted from a variety of public sources.[1]

1. Never use a big word when a diminutive alternative would suffice.

2. Avoid Alliteration. Always.

3. Prepositions are not words to end sentences with.

4. Avoid clichés like the plague. (They're old hat.)

5. It behooves you to avoid archaic expressions.

6. If any word is improper at the end of a sentence, a linking verb is.

7. Parenthetical remarks (however relevant) are unnecessary.

8. It is wrong to ever split an infinitive.

9. Contractions aren't necessary.

10. Foreign words and phrases are not apropos.

11. One should never generalize.

[1] A majority of the sources are from www.plainlanguage.gov prior to the latest website revision.

12. Eliminate quotations. As Ralph Waldo Emerson once said, "I hate quotations. Tell me what you know."

13. Comparisons are as bad as clichés.

14. Don't be redundant; don't use more words than necessary; it's superfluous.

15. Profanity sucks.

16. Be more or less specific.

17. The word *the* is the most overused word in the English language.

18. The passive voice is to be avoided.

19. Exaggeration is a billion times worse than understatement.

20. One word sentences? Eliminate.

21. Analogies in writing are like feathers on a snake.

22. Proofread carefully to see if you any words out.

23. Even if a mixed metaphor sings, it should be derailed.

24. Who needs rhetorical questions?

25. Make this your number one guiding principle write short, simple sentences rather than running on and on and not getting to the point since your reader's attention is fleeting and you don't want to lose them in rambling paragraph-length jumbles that are hard to understand or even comprehend and after all simplicity is the key.

26. Eschew obfuscation.

27. Adverbs really suck.

28. Don't repeat yourself, or say again what you have said before.

29. As I told my wife, don't interject personal matters in objective writing.

30. I never use the first person singular. I think it shows self-absorption.

31. Don't you get tired of writers who think they can sound like Andy Rooney? I know I do. What's with them, anyway?

32. As Bill Safire told me, don't name-drop!

33. As a general rule, don't start sentences with introductory phrases.

34. Avoid Biz-speak. Going forward, empower yourself to write "outside the box".

35. Quotation marks have only one legitimate use: to "indicate" when something is an exact quote.

36. And always be sure to finish what

> **TIP: Read the proposal aloud during the final review. This seemingly mind numbing activity will catch many subtle errors. Just make sure you do not ask the same people to do it every time.**

The Stealth Assassin

In 2009, a major car manufacturer suffered the largest automotive recall in history. Their cars worked well, reliably, safely, economically, and serviceably. A primary problem: floor mats interfering with gas pedals. The manufacturer did not even make the mats.

A simple flaw hidden in the complex process of creating modern automobiles undid the quality reputation the manufacturer had diligently built over decades. Creating proposals that respond to government solicitations is also complex.

Error #11

Hard coding cell values in electronic spreadsheets

Electronic proposal submission is the norm for presenting complex data. Your proposal will likely include data in a spreadsheet format. Data is not limited to cost volumes but is peppered throughout many technical and managerial volumes.

The term hard coding is the insertion of the numerical value rather than allowing the calculated numerical result to show. It replaces the formula.

Do not hard code cells in electronic spreadsheets.

You may believe that inserting the number rather than retaining the underlying formulas will ensure that no errors are made in handling or transmitting your information. This bad idea comes from the fear that information might be changed in electronic transmission. This fear is an artifact from a bygone era.

Evaluation teams often rely on sophisticated analysis software, which requires loading your information for processing. They use these types of software for many purposes including performing cost comparisons, validating component comparisons, cross checking personnel elements, and should-cost analyses.

If you hard-code results in lieu of formulas in your spreadsheets, you have introduced an additional complication to the evaluation process. Rather than reducing the potential for errors you have introduced more latent opportunities for errors as the evaluators must now make assumptions about the formulas. At a minimum, you have made the overworked evaluator less productive and, at worst, made their perceptions unfavorable.

The subliminal message is much more serious. If the evaluator sees your spreadsheets do not contain the formulas, but only inserted values, they may suspect that your values are not correct. This leads to a misgiving that more spreadsheet values may be incorrect. You have introduced a suspicion that your spreadsheet has been manipulated to hide a deficiency or inflate an advantage. This leads to trust and creditability issues: a serious disadvantage to your company and damaging to your reputation.

Keep formulas. It prevents manual interventions in automated evaluation software.

Clearly direct that hard coding spreadsheet cells is unacceptable and reinforce it in your quality control processes. Failure to do so will almost certainly frustrate a sophisticated evaluator. The evaluator may unleash his or her creative genius to find ways to mark your proposal as high risk or noncompliant. Chalk up another loss in your Win/Loss column.

TIP: Instruct your technical editors to use the formula auditing functions of electronic spreadsheets to check for these errors.

Gushing Vomitus

When you write a good resume, you succinctly illustrate your achievements in order to match your skills and experiences to a potential opportunity. You emphasize those experiences that relate well to a prospective job opening and downplay or omit those that are not relevant. You are defining yourself in writing to the hiring manager. Like a hiring manager, a proposal evaluator is analyzing whether or not to hire your company to complete a contract.

Evaluators are busy people trying to do a good job quickly. Anything that distracts from that objective lowers their perception of your company. If you gush, you come crashing down from the lofty pedestal upon which you desire to be viewed. More significantly, information that was not requested can work against you.

Error #12

Submitting information that wasn't requested

If, for example, you proudly cite a successfully completed contract that is not included in your contract references, you create a potential liability. The government has the right to review performance on the non-referenced contract. You have put it forward to be verified and potentially evaluated through input given by someone you did not list as a point of contact. You have introduced a distraction and increased the evaluator's workload. This is in direct opposition to your interests.

A second situation occurs when a proposal manager pastes words from a previously successful proposal into a current one. The information you present must be clearly relevant to the topic at hand or it similarly works against you. Perceptions are created in the evaluators' minds of a rote and largely irrelevant response. Although the prose may glow, irritation also grows.

Gushing behavior can be traced to corporate conceit. Someone in the proposal management process has misplaced corporate pride. The result comes across as an unattractive boast. Evaluators can conclude your company wants them only to read your impressive write-up but not verify your facts. Trust me: they will not be impressed.

Writing a proposal is all about responding in a compelling manner to the customer's requirements. The narrative is not about everything your company does or has done. Leave that role to your marketing department.

Failure to control proposal content is risky. Gushing vomitus is often detected by a serious difficulty in maintaining the proposal page counts.

TIP: Beware of the tendency to cut and paste mindlessly from other proposals or insert unneeded corporate boilerplate.

Don't Bring a Knife to a Gunfight

Mismatches create discontinuities in expectations. A good comedian works tirelessly to create the precise form, cultural context, timing, and language of his art. Out of the blue elements are weaved into a discontinuity of thought to create wonderful comedy. However, discontinuities in the narrative flow of your description of your corporate ability to perform well on contracts do not work in your favor.

Your past performance submissions must facilitate a smooth proposal flow. They must match the expectations of the evaluators.

Cited past performance contracts must be relevant.

Error #13

Not carefully choosing and citing proper past performances

Regardless of glowing corporate mythology about performance on a particular contract, past performance citations must add value to the current solicitation response. If they do not, strike them and get others. Irrelevant past performance references to a current solicitation are inappropriate and distracting.

Consider several facets when selecting appropriate past performances to submit for each proposal. Citing a government contract always weighs more heavily in evaluations than a commercial contract. Contract performance on government work is easier for evaluators to validate using government databases. Most government contracts are framed in similar contract language. The listed point of contact is usually a government person for whom proposal evaluators give instant, ironclad credibility.

Some potential past performance reference contracts can cause visceral distress on the part of the government's evaluation team. This reaction occurs from obviously inappropriate comparisons, such as reference contracts with no relevance to the current solicitation. This situation may occur when potential subcontractors submit proposal reference contracts through primes. If the prime has not clearly outlined what the subcontractor is expected to accomplish, the relevance of the reference contract is difficult to determine.

View your past performance reference contracts from the perspective of an

Your control methods to accept or reject past performance contracts should be rigorous. Objectivity becomes difficult when reviewing your own corporate references. Be equally critical of the applicability of your own references as you are of your subcontractors' references.

In addition to selecting past performances with the proper relevance, critically review your performance on them from the government's perspective. The government Contractor Performance Assessment Reporting System (CPARS) contains performance information on your prior government contracts. CPARS are accessible to the government and to the performing contractor. You can check on how the government scored your performance. The evaluators will certainly check them.

In many cases, you can use the information contained within the CPARS to strengthen your case. A good CPARS rating is a fact based validation of your strong capabilities of contract performance. A poor CPARS rating is a strong incentive for you to eliminate a particular contract as a reference for proposals.

Your past performance volume manager should have well defined criteria for the inclusion or rejection of past performance contracts.

> **TIP: You can access CPARS information in the Past Performance Information Retrieval System (PPIRS.) Information in the PPIRS is kept on file for three years after contract completion.**

> **TIP: Once your CPARS information is posted, download your own copy of it to be able to quote it even after it has expired from the government site.**

PART 4 - ERRORS REVEALING PATHETIC PLANNING

Proposal writing, which is the focus of this book, is just one element in the overall process of sustaining work for your employees. Integrate proposal planning with the larger business development and capture planning processes.

A key element in planning is a structured review process. These are often called Color Team reviews. These reviews encompass more than just the proposal process. Processes and reviews should all be consistent for your company.

If your company is perceived as unable to adequately plan and submit a proposal, the government will be justifiably skeptical about your corporate ability to perform on the contract. Your business reputation will be negatively impacted.

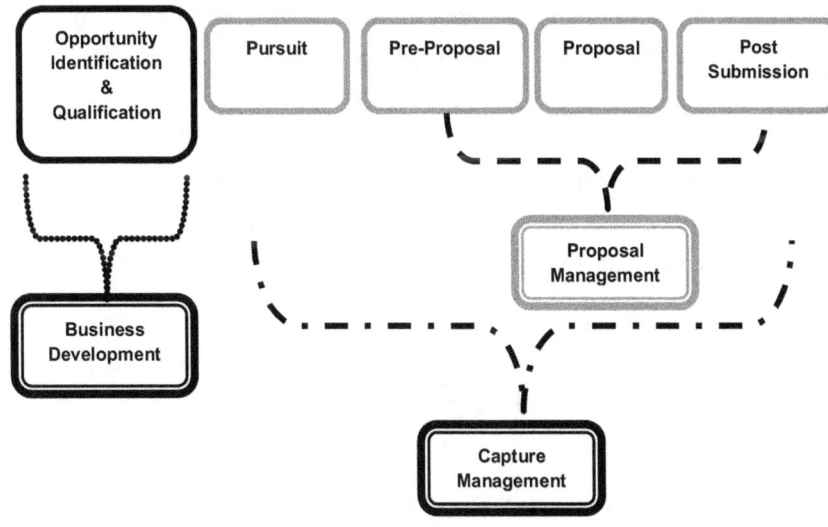

Unpolished Diamonds

The difference between success and failure is not adherence to the idea of "good enough." When you envisage a high profile Madison Avenue marketing firm, one of your mental images might be of highly polished advertising. The finished products are typically flawless. They must represent the image of the advertising agency's clients. They have been conceived, fleshed out, scripted, produced, and published. They are edited for many significant variables. The reason all of these expensive actions are undertaken is because they work toward the ultimate success of the product being sold and the reputation of the company selling the product.

The failure to do a comprehensive edit can relate directly to your corporate reputation. How well your proposal team executes the proposal is an indication to the government of your ability to professionally execute a resulting contract. The submitted proposal quality, its completeness, focus, organization, and style, is the source selection team's persuasive indicator of competence. A final comprehensive edit ensures all requested information is presented professionally.

Error #14

Failure to do a comprehensive edit

To edit means a wide range of correcting, condensing, choosing, modifying, and changing. These essential activities are trivialized in the minds of some editors into exclusively concentrating on correct placement of punctuation.

Overall impact and appearance are important. Proposal appearance is more than graphics. Your proposal document should be professional. The final product must be free of typos, blank pages, unnumbered pages, smudges, unintended whitespace, sloppy-looking pages, poor graphics, and much more.

Proposals exclusively submitted electronically and those submitted on paper have subtle but important differences. A professional editor can assist you.

Your proposal manager is responsible to do a content edit to avoid omitting key elements in the solicitation response. This type of edit is different for varying proposal types. For example, some short form or task order proposals neglect to explain how or by whom the project will be managed. This is the primary purpose of the management volume in a larger proposal, but it might not be explicitly requested in more limited solicitation forms.

> *The purpose of an edit is your message readability and comprehension.*

Omit essential management information at your grave risk. Evaluators who were not part of the original master contract often do short form or task order proposal evaluations. They may need a quick reminder of certain facts contained in the master contract to give you your best chance of winning the task order.

The issue of relevancy highlighted in the past performance contracts discussion applies to other proposal elements. The fact that in your Karachi office you have a terrific process for repairing diesel engines does not go far in convincing an evaluation team that you have the best capabilities toward an IT Systems Engineering contract in Des Moines. *All information* in the proposal relative to your firm, your management and staff, and your capabilities *must be relevant.*

Your proposal should include your specific approach to the project. You unique approach should be, after all, why you are proposing to this RFP in the first place. Some companies generate multiple proposals in an assembly line fashion in the hope that something will result in a contract award. This runs the risk of addressing requirements generically, rather than specifically. Hope is not an effective strategy.

If your message is lost, it doesn't matter if your grammar, usage, and punctuation are exquisite. Your written proposal has multiple evaluation objectives. It creates messages in addition to evaluation scores. It projects an image of your company's capability and quality. This projection is translated into risk scores, which heavily influence the overall evaluation.

> *An edit is both an action and a process.*

Evaluators and contracting officers award to companies exhibiting high competence and low risk, as well as, good value. Ensure your proposal quality reflects those messages.

Plan your proposal quality control milestones and observe them conscientiously. Some companies rely on only one superficial quality milestone, usually a red team review. This examines and reviews their proposal, the one and only time, prior to submitting it to the government. This is a mistake. Quality control is an essential thread throughout the proposal process and more than one review is required.

Your proposal must demonstrate that your company has the capability to carry out the solicitation requirements successfully. This is a direct evaluation issue. A good proposal will also address the evaluation team's implicit questions.

Thoroughly edit your proposal so it can do its job effectively. Your professional reputation is not well served if your proposal is poorly written, unorganized, filled with grammatical errors, and difficult to follow.

TIP: Engage a proposal manager who is also an experienced writer and appreciates the encompassing nature of a professional edit.

The ADHD Syndrome

There is a spring in your step. Imagine yourself walking into a sleek Silicon Valley office of a highly successful information technology firm on a bright sunny morning. You are a venture capitalist being courted to invest significant funds in a firm's breakthrough innovation, which provides a highly efficient method of analyzing energy production from wind turbine farms. The innovation allows the turbine blades of individual units to adjust as a function of both the overall wind farm output and the efficiency of individual turbines. This information and coordinated management subsequently optimizes the production of the entire farm instead of individual turbines. It has the potential to increase wind farm output by double-digit percentages. The market and profit impacts are potentially huge.

Error #15

Writing in a disconnected and random manner

As you listen to the presentation, you start to realize that the information is being presented in an ad-hoc manner. As you struggle to relate technologies with production issues and costs with governance practices, you start to perceive that there is more risk with the company and venture than you previously anticipated. Your initial positive feeling becomes increasingly uncomfortable due to the disorganized manner in which the information is being presented. You evaluate the opportunity as too risky for proper execution by the firm.

Failure to have a consistent theme in your proposal diminishes your corporate credibility. Random writing is like telling a story with no plot. The narrative fails to imprint a message.

It is not enough to just acknowledge a proposal requirement. It needs to be incorporated into the solution. Some proposals write voluminously about requirements, but fail to provide solutions for them. This error is more common than one might believe. Some writers wander around a requirement but fail to provide an adequate solution. Requirements must be addressed as part of the overall proposal flow and be part of the solution.

Poor proposal planning and the resultant wandering narrative often result from a lack of an easily accessible storyboard to which all capture team and proposal team members can frequently refer. It might seem strange to the uninitiated to have the word *storyboard* in the same context as a response to a solicitation or RFP, but some form of storyboarding or document planning is essential.

> *If you cannot clearly and logically describe how you intend to perform on the contract, you introduce more risk into the minds of the evaluators.*

Your proposal describes to the government how you intend to fulfill the solicitation's requirements. Your proposal is the cogent, organized, and convincing explanation of your ideas to the various evaluators. It asserts, promotes, and justifies your superior ability to execute on the contract above all other competitors.

A well-written proposal has a unifying proposition that ties the entire document together. This overall unifying proposition must be iterated and supported throughout the proposal with themes addressing major requirements of the solicitation. The themes in turn must logically be supported by facts and findings, highlighting benefits to the government. This turns your unique qualifications and capabilities into a coherent and logical story line.

Writing a reputation enhancing response emphasizes a consistent thread of coherent ideas and due respect for the evaluation criteria and weighting. One useful method is to segregate the win theme into its supporting themes and elements. Then show why they are supportive. Every supporting theme must match a major requirement of the solicitation. In every proposal, carefully weave together the reasons why your company's solution is better than

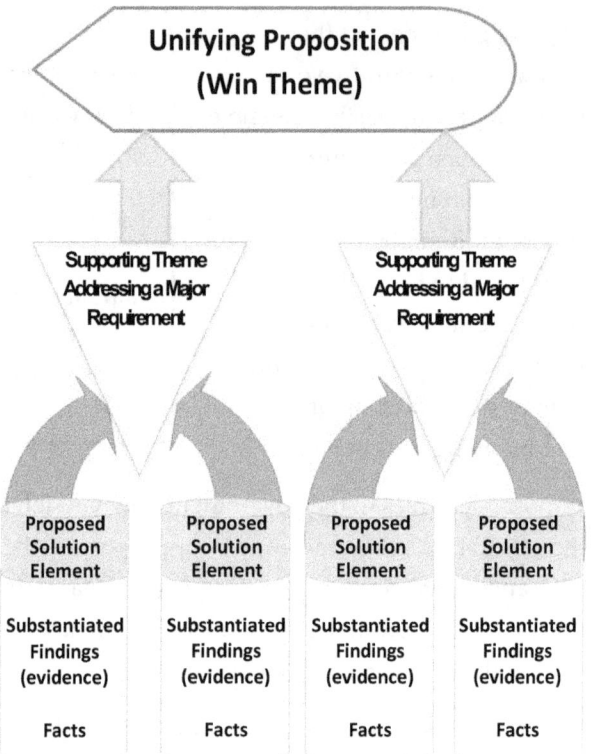

all others and, importantly, how your solution satisfies the requirements of the solicitation. A good rule of thumb is to have no more than three to five win themes.

Buttress supporting themes with proposed solution elements that are in turn standing firmly on facts and substantiated findings. While this may seem to be a bit formulaic to those who are not experienced proposal writers, it becomes second nature to those who do this routinely, and **WIN**.

A danger of a large proposal is that the many details of writing the various volumes become very complex. It becomes difficult to keep the main flow of ideas intact. This danger can be reduced in proposal preparation by a short synopsis sent to members of the proposal writing team and executive management. This synopsis includes the win theme.

However, an error occurs when a company falls in love with a clever win theme that overshadows your ability and willingness to perform the solicitation's stated requirements. Writers start to wax eloquently about a theme, and they forget the reality that the government does not award contracts based upon win themes. Evaluation teams evaluate the proposal capabilities, features, benefits, costs, and risks. A good win theme merely puts these factors into an easily understood thematic context. Your proposal becomes more memorable which reinforces your message of competence.

Your reputation is damaged if evaluators get lost reading your proposal. Subconsciously, they start to equate your company with distraction and risk. Failure to write consistently throughout the proposal raises risk alerts to the evaluation team. After all, if you can't even manage to put together a coherent and comprehensible response to a solicitation, how can you be expected to manage an awarded contract?

> **TIP: ALWAYS do a proposal plan. Failure to plan is inevitably a failure to perform.**

> **TIP: Have your proposal manager develop a one-half page elevator speech about the unique benefits of your proposal. This keeps the unifying proposition in context for writers.**

Blindly Sailing into Uncharted Waters

Are you trying to interpret coffee stains on a map? Understanding intents and meanings in a government solicitation might be similar. You may arrive at the wrong conceptual destination. For example, your interpretation of the definition of a *socio-anthropologically accurate terrain map* might be fraught with misunderstandings. The combination of elements in a solicitation can create questions. A striking example came from a solicitation from a research and development agency that required everyone, including administrative and janitorial personnel, to be qualified nuclear engineers. REALLY?!

Ask questions!

Some companies are reluctant to ask questions. Failure to clarify solicitation language and intent indicates poor proposal management. Seek interpretation and guidance. Avoiding ambiguity is clearly in your company's best interest.

Error #16

Failure to ask questions early in the process

Reluctance to ask questions is avoidance behavior. It may result from pressure to get other jobs done. It can also result from a belief that one's assumptions are correct. Failure to ask questions early in the process can be a serious tactical error. Often several opportunities occur in the capture process to get answers prior to the RFP release. The earlier you clearly understand requirements, context, and intent, the higher your chances of a successful bid. If you have questions after the draft RFP is issued, you have the right to submit those questions in writing to the Contracting Officer. There is no penalty, real or perceived, for asking well thought-out questions.

Most RFP's specify a question submission deadline. Ensure your proposal team collects the questions and submits them as early as possible, but always before the deadline date. Early question submissions usually prompt a quicker government response.

There is always a consideration of fair competition in every communication from the government. As such, all responses to submitted questions are distributed to all bidders. The responses may be delivered through a solicitation addendum or amendment or by posting a series of questions and answers separately.

Some question submission deadlines are quite early in the draft proposal process.

Questions should be asked if they can be classified in one of two ways.

1. Do you need to know this information in order to bid?
2. Do you need clarification.

The way you frame your questions is important. Although you and your firm will not be identified with specific questions, the way you word your questions could provide important information to your competitors. Phrase your questions carefully to ensure that you will not give away information about your strategy or assumptions.

Review your questions. Then vet your questions internally before submitting them to the government. One method that works well is to create a two or three person panel. The panel should then jointly review potential questions. The review should concentrate on three primary issues.

1. **Is the question truly not answered within the entire RFP?** Asking a needless question damages your reputation.

2. Is the question an issue of interpretation? Requesting a clarification of an interpretation is often better than asking for a direct answer to a question. This illustrates that your company gave considerable thought to the issue.

3. Does asking the question reveal important information about your corporate strategy? It might be better to wait for a less sophisticated competitor to ask. If not asked by a competitor, then deal with the issue in the most conservative interpretation.

Many questions should and must be asked. After you determine a question is truly worthwhile, you should next consider phrasing. If possible, phrase questions fashioned so that the answer may better position your solution.

Some solicitations have obvious discontinuities. The government agency's drafting process may take cut and paste shortcuts from one solicitation to another. A striking example of this came from an agency solicitation for information technology management and analysis support that included the following: "The contractor shall provide underwater salvage, repair, and maintenance operation services and support."

The failure to ask a question that should be asked can damage your reputation as much as asking a question inappropriately.

> **TIP:** Attend every industry day, or have a trusted and knowledgeable third party attend on your behalf. Many questions are answered in detail, in public.

Finish Line Tripping

Do you watch track and field? Relay races highlight the contributions of each team member, as well as, the performance of the entire team. There is a clear team conclusion: win, lose, or draw. There is thrilling competitiveness and determined effort at every stage of the race by the runners. You see the smooth handoffs and determine which team has exhaustively practiced the art of passing the baton. The team strategy is based on highlighting an individual's best features for the team's benefit.

Error #17

Failure to deliver the proposal on time

The most heartbreaking event, and one that destroys the team's great performance, is when the anchor runner, in a desperate effort to win, overextends and trips just before the finish line. You don't often remember the name of the anchor runner, but vividly recall *the team* that failed spectacularly.

Failure to deliver on time is almost always a failure to plan or a failure to stick to the plan. The proposal plan should be constructed by starting from the submission date and time, then working generously backwards to the appropriate milestone dates.

Quality production takes time.

Do not underestimate the time it takes to accomplish professional copy production. People who are not in the production process often discount these tasks and the times required. They usually presume both priority and ability to turn around documents in a flash. They do not presume balky printers, power outages, overturned coffee cups, or internet calamity.

Proposal managers should discuss production department timelines and workload to ensure ample and realistic time frames.

Then they should periodically validate that the circumstances remain favorable. The time it takes to produce the final products will vary depending upon the media type: hardcopy, electronic, CDs/DVDs, and the assembly leading to a professional product.

Prepare a final production plan. Integrate it into the proposal master plan. Make sure all team members clearly understand the parameters, schedule deadlines, and materials required.

A common planning error is failure to identify clearly the person responsible for delivery. Require the proposal delivery person to provide a delivery plan with contingency options. This straightforward requirement has the additional benefit of jump-starting his or her planning thought process. When you require a plan, you also highlight that delivery planning has management attention.

> *Prepare a final production plan and integrate it into the master plan.*

Some companies routinely send two or three proposal originals by different means, routes, and methods. These include: hand carried with a driver; FED-EX or UPS; bicycle messenger; print at a distant location close to the delivery site; and many other variations.

Senior managers are sometimes the fatal flaw in process control. If they are only involved at the end, they may destroy the timeline with last-minute changes. This disrupts schedules and turns orderly events into chaotic disarray. The result is a finish line failure.

> **TIP: Have your own proof of proper delivery. A simple signed receipt with a time/date is sufficient.**

PART 5 - A MOUNTAINTOP VIEW

In my office hangs calligraphy presented to me by a Japanese admiral. He presented it to me with the words, "The view is farthest from the top of the mountain." As the owner and leader of your company, your view should be the most encompassing and visionary. Your reputation is your most valuable asset as a contractor. Your proposal will either cloud your business reputation or brighten it.

Professional proposal planning, execution, and submission are extensions of your corporate image. Your client communications should emulate the sophistication of your products and services. They build your reputation, or sink it.

This book seeks to stimulate your thoughts about your business's proposal preparation process and provoke action toward improvement. Does your management team execute as professionally as it should? Should you call on independent assistance to make your proposals professional?

Don't let these 17 common errors sink your business reputation. You control your destiny. Your proposal can enhance your business reputation. Pay attention to this most important communication you provide to your government customer — the proposal.

It's your company. It's your reputation It's your success..

APPENDICIES

Appendix A: Federal Contract Format [1]

The Uniform Contract Format is organized into parts and sections:

PART ONE – THE SCHEDULE

Section A – Solicitation and Contract Form

Section B - Supplies or Services and Prices/Costs

Section C - Description/Specification/Work Statement

Section D –Packaging and Marking

Section E – Inspection and Acceptance

Section F – Deliveries or Performance

Section G – Contract Administration Data

Section H – Special Contract Clauses

PART TWO – CONTRACT CLAUSES

Section I – Contract Clauses

PART THREE – LIST OF DOCUMENTS, EXHIBITS, AND OTHER ALTERNATIVES

Section J – List of Attachments

PART FOUR – REPRESENTATIONS AND CERTIFICATIONS

Section K – Representations and Certifications and Other Statements of Offerors

Section L – Instructions, Conditions and Notices of Offerors

Section M – Evaluation Factors for Award

---

1. Federal Acquisition Regulations (FAR 1.4201.1

Appendix B: Terms and Definitions [1]

Types of Plans

Account Plan

A sales plan that is specific to one particular customer and will cover multiple opportunities with that customer. It typically covers 2-5 years.

Capture Plan

The accumulated and documented analysis, strategies and actions initiated following the pursuit decision that details customer issues, considerations relating to competition and internal positioning, approaches and management tasks to be used to guide the capture of a specific opportunity.

Proposal Outline Plan

A structure for the proposal that is usually derived from the customer's requirements documentation. It may be annotated to show writing assignments, estimates etc.

Proposal Resource Schedule

A task based plan that identifies the period of time that work is required against each task.

Progress and/or Decision point reviews: often called Color Team reviews

Opportunity Identification Review

The initial decision point of opportunity suitability.

Pursuit Decision Point

Establish the priority of various valid opportunities.

---

[1] Association of Proposal Management Professionals, APMP Accreditation Glossary, dated 2/4/2009.

Bid/No Bid Review

Corporately ascertain willingness to allocate bid and proposal resources.

Capture Strategy Review

Approves the decision to prime/subcontract and overall capture plan.

Proposal Strategy Review

Validate a proposal win strategy.

Competition Review

Formally analyze the expected competition relative to your strengths and vulnerabilities.

Initial Draft Review

Confirm the writers have integrated the strategy and proposal guidance into the initial writing.

Final Draft Review

Evaluate the proposal against criteria relative to customer focus, completeness, and clear communication of your solutions and benefits (commonly called a red team review).

Overall Bid Review

This is the final review prior to submission to confirm your offer entails acceptable profit and risk.

Lessons Learned review

A review to determine how processes, strategies and approaches can be improved.

Proposal Tools

Bidders Comparison Matrix

A tool used to compare a potential offer against possible competing offers as judged by the customer.

Compliance Checklists

A list of specific customer requirements. The list is often generated by splitting complex questions into separate requirements.

Compliance Matrix

Also called a response matrix. The matrix is a road map that enables the evaluator to use it as a reference that points to a specific proposal response for each compliance item.

Proposal Responsibility Matrix

A matrix that identifies team members with specific proposal sections responsibility.

Requirements checklist

Similar to a compliance checklist but can be self-generated when there is not written customer requirement. It is often used as tool to monitor progress.

Storyboard

Conceptual planning tool used to help writers plan each section before drafting text; contains assignments, bid request requirements, strategies, preliminary visuals and contents.

Work Breakdown Structure

Deliverable-oriented grouping of project elements that organizes and defines the total work scope of the project; each descending level represents an increasingly detailed definition of the project work.

Responsibilities Identification:

Capture Manager

Leads entire capture team. Capture manager responsibilities extend across the Pre-bid, Bid and Post-bid phases of a capture opportunity.

Contractual Volume Leader

Identifies, organizes, and directs contracts, legal and purchasing personnel to complete the contractual response.

Delivery Leader

Responsible for all aspects of delivery including identifying, organizing, and directing program management, order and billing, engineering, installation, documentation, training and O&M personnel to complete the proposal delivery response.

Pricing Leader

Identifies, organizes and directs pricing personnel to complete the proposal pricing response.

Proposal Manager

Person responsible for proposal development, including maintaining schedules; coordinating inputs, reviews, strategy implementation; resolving internal problems; and providing process leadership.

Sales Leader

Acts as the customer surrogate during proposal construction. Leads completion of competitive assessments, usually writes the executive summary first draft, primary developer of win themes and strategy.

Technical Leader

Identifies, organizes and directs personnel to design the solution and complete the proposal technical response.

Federal Government definitions[1]:

Solicitation

Means any request to submit offers or quotations to the Government.

> Solicitations under sealed bid procedures are called *"invitations for bids."*

> Solicitations under negotiated procedures are called *"requests for proposals."*

> Solicitations under simplified acquisition procedures may require submission of either *a quotation or an offer.*

Task order

Means an order for services placed against an established contract or with Government source.

Unsolicited proposal

Means a written proposal for a new or innovative idea that is submitted to an agency on the initiative of the offeror for the purpose of obtaining a contract with the Government, and that is not in response to a request for proposal.

---

[1] Federal Acquisition regulations Part 2

ATTACHMENTS

Attachment A: Quick Error Checklist

Error #1 - Not truly understanding your audience

Error #2 - Failure to succinctly answer why YOUR company above all others

Error #3 - Failure to weight evaluation criteria properly

Error #4 - Unprofessional writing

Error #5 - Not providing a unique, compelling solution

Error #6 - Not validating past performance points of contact

Error #7 - Not responding to specific directions in the proposal

Error #8 - Exceeding page count limits

Error #9 - Putting pricing related info into inappropriate volumes

Error #10 - Depending on spell-check to ensure correct grammar and usage

Error #11 - Hard coding cell values in electronic spreadsheets

Error #12 - Submitting information that wasn't requested

Error #13 - Not carefully choosing and citing proper past performances

Error #14 - Failure to do a comprehensive edit

Error #15 - Writing in a disconnected and random manner

Error #16 - Failure to ask questions early in the process

Error #17 - Failure to deliver the proposal on time

Attachment B: Writer's Guide Elements

The proposal guide can be a simple slide deck. Technical personnel are often quite visually oriented, so having a writers guide in presentation software slides tends to make them more readily identify with the concepts of the guide. At a minimum, the following elements should be included in a writers guide.

- The win theme on the cover slide
- General writing guidelines including ideas that are presented in this book
- A decomposition of the win theme broken out into relevant points pertaining to each proposal volume
- The volume and section page limits for each element of the proposal
- The evaluation factors with their relative merit
- Technical page guidance, including instructions on tables, matrices, classification guidelines, charts and graphs
- Example of the cross reference matrix with each of the constituent parts and examples if necessary
- Risk identification and mitigation strategies
- Guidelines for electronic media including embedded and attached items
- Discriminator elements and how they are to be integrated into the proposal (one slide for each element)
- Alignments and linkages to items supporting the solicitation, such as statements of objectives or technical references
- Discussion of each unique element highlighted in the proposal such as unusual corporate qualifications, changes to the contracting method from previous contracts, etc.
- Technical production guidance

ABOUT THE AUTHOR

Alan L. Heisig AM.APMP is an executive advisor and accredited proposal manager. He is one a small cadre of professionals worldwide accredited through the Association of Proposal Management Professionals for both public and private proposal management.

He has had a distinguished career in the federal services industry as an operational enterprise vice president, proposal manager and business developer. He is a former US Navy Captain, a commodore, and captain of multiple ships and an information technology professional. His highly successful active duty concluded on the Joint Chiefs of Staff, as the Deputy Director for Defense Wide Command, Control, Computers and Communications.

Alan is a sought after speaker, and senior proposal consultant to companies that provide products and services to the federal government. His clients include several of the top ten defense contractors and many mid-tier and smaller companies.

Learn more about his company on the web at _www.alansaglobal.com_

DEDICATION

This book is dedicated to our unique national treasure: our servicemen and servicewomen who selflessly and dedicatedly protect our country and its freedoms.

Join the volunteers who assist those wounded in the service of our country, our wounded United States Soldiers, Sailors, Airmen, Marines, Coast Guardsmen and Merchant Mariners. Our country owes them a debt of gratitude that is within our capability to assist in repaying. That repayment is to assist them in overcoming the obstacles they encounter as a result of their service.

Please consider getting involved with the Wounded Warrior Project whose mission is to honor and empower wounded warriors.

These men and women deserve an opportunity to pursue meaningful lives as productive members of American society. They have given so much to ensure the maintenance of our freedoms.

The purpose of the Wounded Warrior project is threefold:

> To raise awareness and enlist the public's aid for the needs of severely injured service men and women,
>
> To help severely injured service members aid and assist each other, and
>
> Provide unique, direct programs and services to meet the needs of severely injured service members.

Please visit
http://www.woundedwarriorproject.org

Find a program or project that fits your ability.

Take action. Employ wounded warriors.

* 9 7 8 1 4 6 6 2 5 9 0 7 2 *